ALARUM

Wayne Holloway-Smith was born in Wiltshire and lives in London. He received his PhD in English and Creative Writing from Brunel University in 2015. His poems have appeared in many magazines and anthologies. His pocketbook, *Beloved, in case you've been wondering*, was published by Donut Press in 2011. He co-edits the online journal *Poems in Which* and teaches at the University of Hertfordshire. His first book-length collection *Alarum* was published by Bloodaxe in 2017.

WAYNE HOLLOWAY-SMITH

Alarum

BLOODAXE BOOKS

Copyright © Wayne Holloway-Smith 2017

ISBN: 978 1 78037 330 0

First published 2017 by
Bloodaxe Books Ltd
Eastburn
South Park
Hexham
Northumberland NE46 1BS

www.bloodaxebooks.com
For further information about Bloodaxe titles
please visit our website or write to
the above address for a catalogue.

Supported using public funding by
**ARTS COUNCIL
ENGLAND**

Printed in Great Britain by Bell & Bain Limited, Glasgow, Scotland, on
acid-free paper sourced from mills with FSC chain of custody certification.

for Sarah and Margot

ACKNOWLEDGEMENTS

With thanks to the following publications where a number of these poems, or earlier versions of them, have been included: *Best British Poetry 2013* (Salt Publishing, 2013), *Birdbook 3* (Sidekick Books, 2015), *BroadCast, City State: New London Poetry* (Penned in the Margins, 2008), *Erotic Review, Oxford Poetry, Peony Moon, Poems in Which, Poetry, Poetry London* and *The Poetry Review.*

With love and thanks to Jack Underwood, Alex MacDonald, Annie Freud, Heather Phillipson, Amy Key, Rebecca Perry, Mark Waldron, Joe Dunthorne, Kate Kilalea, Holly Pester, Andy Ching, Claire Lynch, HUSK for the writer's residency, The Society of Authors for an Arthur Fenton Award, Roddy Lumsden, Ahren Warner and Emily Berry.

CONTENTS

I

The air itself

inside the tiny, inside the candy-coloured theatre,
open to the beachfront, sweet to the retina
and wriggling, you might say, in the palaver of its excess,
is suddenly still as the found-out devil,
it's a drunk man discovered by the frightening silence of morning,
or it's a sneaking crocodile caught with a sausage in its muzzle,
or it's the reality of silence – that part of a child's face
when its ice cream slips from the cone. It's trapped, the air is,
as perpetual rudeness is trapped in the dead slap
of a flat stick, the very second it's rapped, the exact
second it's given to the head of its pinstriped, its pinnied victim – oh Judy!
– and it's staid, like the violence of a tossed-up baby,
or the shadow, the mournful shadow of a man –
its penumbra of bent nose and sticky-out chin – slow-rocking
and almost kazoo-like in its shrill and *don't-blame-me* fauna,
while respectable mothers do pick up their infants,
while husbands do throw an implicit arm over the wife's shoulder,
as grandparents, swathed in sun cream, do ease their deckchairs shut
and everything just sort of creeps soft and backwards,
as the sea creeps, in out-roads of awkwardness.
It's whispering, the air is, as the sand here might whisper:
I don't like it anymore, please, for God's sake, take me with you.

If I forget this, let my tongue cling to the roof of my mouth

Another thing I'm learning is that heartbreak is recycled
like rain is recycled
it's raining and I don't want it to   that pop stars use up
all the rain singing   but it still comes back again
every time adultery happens or a girl with blue eyes
or somewhere my father dies.
Everything is sometimes broken   except you
always working on a building site   you eating beef sandwiches
and swearing.

There is so much ground everywhere but rain manages
to find you inside your tiny part of it.
If this were a song I would add another instrument here
I would have dancers when I sing it   a band.
Remember when I threw myself in the air
    Dad   it was raining
and I said catch it was raining   you were gone.
Actually   you were watching the news.

Another thing I've learned is   look out of the window.
On building sites all over the world   pop stars in tiny radios.
On building sites the weather's bad and stacks of men
have their backs to it.

If this were a song I'd sing it all over those building sites
until I found you then I'd sing it
on your building site like a singer singing
about heartbreak   and it's raining
and there are lots of dancers behind in dresses
the dresses getting see-through then the dancers
are getting see-through and the backing band
and their instruments. You see

how empty this all is how meaningless
without the dressing   the singer is just mouthing words
    we hated each other didn't we
even when the music's stopped and it's just rain
and my hands up my sleeves

Some Waynes

Magic Wayne with flowers; Wanye West; Box-of-Tricks Wayne;
Wayne sad on Facebook, proving he loves his daughter; the
sporty Wayne – loves himself skinny; Bald Wayne, head like a
rocking chair; Amy Waynehouse; Wayne the ironic; Fat Wayne
– tits pushed beneath a Fred Perry Wayne; Wayne from near
Slough; Ugly Wayne – the unlikely mess of his wife Wayne –
canned laughter; Wayne who renamed another Wayne fleabag;
Track-suited Wayne – your hubcaps, his pockets; Home and
A-Wayne; Randy Wayne; Wayne, fountains of him, every drop
snug to someone's mum; Wayne, boyfriend of Stacey; Wayne-
ker; Wayne the rap star, gold teeth, grime; Wayne the Superhero;
Wayne the Cowboy; Dancing Wayne – in tights; It's-Wayning-
Men; a cavalcade of Waynes fucking each other up in a Geoff
Hattersley poem – in a pub, in Barnsley; Purple Wayne;
Wayne's World Wayne; Wayne 'Sleng Teng' Smith; A-Wayne
in a Manger; all of them have stopped what they're doing, all
of them divided in two rows and facing each other, all of them,
arms raised, they are linking fingers, all of them: an architrave
through which I celebrate, marching like I am the bridegroom,
grinning like I am the bride

The Warning Notes

A view of things squared by TV;
the collapse of soap scenes, compelled
by *that* music: one note held
long enough for a sense of dread
to build, followed by death, a burst
vessel in a young boy's head, or the news
I'm afraid she'll never dance again.

Those warning notes always pursue and snatch
the addict almost overcoming his vice,
the young couple subverting their struggle.
As I lay beside her that night, a guitar fell
in the room across the stairs and I froze,
    unsure if I should have given up smoking.

Everything is always sometimes broken

Like a man who once said or did or thought an awful thing,
a single crow fell out my mind and landed
at your feet   I couldn't take it back.
Some people have crows, it's no big deal. But it's there on the floor,
I hoped you wouldn't notice, I couldn't take it back,
swooped to hide the awful thing up my sleeve. I thought

I could trust you. It's no big deal, there are people
you can even talk to about this on the telephone. There are still so many
crows up here, I tell them, and they need feeding, constant attention.
Forgive me, there was a time before I spoke of it,
I couldn't kiss anyone, or hold a baby, or eat food – tomato pasta,
say, or falafel – without addressing first each crow in turn.

I don't want to speak about this anymore. Somewhere
there is a park where men – some teenagers, some much older
than teenagers – are doing chin-ups and sit-ups and running
really fast on the spot. Imagine, having the strength to move
all your body mass like that   crows and all.

Whatever light is made of, it's illuminating that crow directly
on the floor and even now holding who we are in its eye. Wait.

*

If you could perhaps take all this and hold it for just a second,
up to the light, whatever it's made of. If we could
be together in the eye of the awful thing, but together.

They sometimes have a different name for the crows,
but they can't all of them be called that. In parks, people running
in vests, walking dogs. Some people can eat

16

and eat all day, then kiss someone. Others are hatching,
their eyes are nests for it. Some people are trying hard
not to let anything out into the daylight. Then,
wait. It's no big deal.

OK, so crows don't exist. But they do tell me things.
They can't speak English, but give an *impression* of sorts,
sometimes several all at once. OK, so telephones
don't exist either. But I didn't make them up.
It's just me and you. Or just me, trying to tell you something.
My sleeves are getting full.

Doo-wop

There are so many things to run
and hurt yourself against.
    Imagine that, for a moment
we're in a time when you've not yet gone
and I'm telling you
sure as men in the fifties sing in high-pitched voices
    that they really do want you to stay, girl.
There are so many ways to perform this genre.
Look shoo I'm bop di wop kicking
    my bare feet about you
against the skirting boards, scuffing my toes
    on the carpet and singing to the music
it's making my manipulative longing for you
– softening it like those men at the key change –
to please not go
    just a little bit longer   under the ground.

(i.m Phillip Thomas)

No Worries

Oh yes, the help you need is strapping, for sure.
It might at any time now pull up outside your door
in its mucky white van, man-arms flush
to the steering wheel; its muscular weight
the only buoyant thing in your hallway,
your kitchen, and stood upright in itself –
full face, a dimple-cheeked, unshaved grin.
Almost a caricature in its self-assuredness,
and, you imagine, shirtless beneath its coveralls.
A well-oiled metal box of fixing tools. For fixing.
A roll-up behind one ear, it promises itself to you,
that everything can definitely be sorted, mate,
the pieces of it all will be cleaned and fitted
back together. Good as new. No worries.
And you want to believe it'll show up this time, at least
you are sure of that, so sure you can hear it whistle.

*   *   *

So Many Different Ways to Talk About the Same Thing

The wooden sound of clocks. Alcohol. Robins
on Christmas cards. This was the winter when everyone
we knew bought a home and was alive in it,
and some went to America, others got checked for cancer
and we discovered we were not the type of people
who would ever truly ride bikes together. My father died
and from nowhere you were asked by an Italian
with long wide-awake hair to be his girlfriend –
he found you on the internet
in another life. As we laughed I came to understand
there are so many different ways to talk about the same thing,
that somehow this early January had chosen to come down different
and the walls beneath the wallpaper
in our rented flat were still there, being the same.

*

As soon as I finished writing that line it rained
for a long while and then stopped. My dad is dead.
If we could only all lie down in zigzags together everything would fit.
People could all stay where they are, right where they are.
Each morning I wake knowing this and other types of truth.
At the key change of a Whitney Houston song
the curtain always closes over the coffin.

*

The window has been shut since forever. The window
used to be sealed with paint, but now we just keep it shut.
Outside, the world is ticking with robins. Inside there is carpet.
An Italian man wants you for himself, but you are here
to stop me saying Fuck out loud at funerals. You are
in the next room right now and everything is dull.

Everyone is somewhere else.

Fuck. *I will always love you.* Fuck. There, I said both of those.
Sometimes I want to tear the wallpaper to see if I'm right.
I'm right. The whole wall is still there.

What Happened Was This

The more she thought the more she thought not of their marriage/ not
of their wedding night/ but of the night before that night/ or at least
what he told of what he did that night and how he didn't/ this she
knew/ have a proper stag but/ this she didn't/ he and his friends
played a large game of tag in which he hid in a park from
his friends for what seemed like two years/ disguised
by the dark and a bush and no one/ not one/ could find him
and as it grew cold he ignored still their calls/ could hear/
found some kind of comfort in hearing/ their calls
so didn't reveal where he was and thought about sleep
and thought about sex but thought he might stay
there forever then he came/ all of a sudden/ to himself/
in one moment/ and sprang out of the bush into the light
of a street lamp/ and thought they'd all hidden
and thought they were playing a trick/ but then
he realised and then/ andthenandthen/ the kick

There is absolutely no way to make this real life interesting

My ostensible father downstairs is sore to the dickens
about everything
no matter: my illness is all right

two fingers up
the throat of itself   nutrients bawling
across the panels of the bathroom
tears backing up in the backs
of its eyes   and desperate   sometimes laughter

As a child my illness had fat thighs and a scar on its lip
that my mother assured me would one day disappear
as a child my illness was trying itself out

holding itself at angles in the mirror
it wanted so much to be the beautiful boy at school
or something very wrapped up and lifted
a wonderful hybrid creature   and dead
almost beneath its blankets
as a child it was wrong in knitwear eating Mars Bars

bowls of ice cream pasta cold beans
bowls of ice cream cold beans Mars Bars

picture this: my illness in a gym
hidden by large men and mirrors
picture this: a field of red flowers

hidden in a field of flowers my illness
dressed in a wide-rimmed straw hat is eating
all the red flowers

Imagine how many surplus
calories you have to eat to gain one pound
said the therapist in her green cardigan

Think back   she said in an attitude of prayer
Allow your inner-child to speak out
she spoke from beneath long orange hair
What is it saying, what do you want to say
Little Illness?

A shadow carefully distinguishes from all of their shadows
when my illness goes with my friends out driving
to the cinema and with popcorn
it is distrustful   of the girl at the counter because maybe
the girl at the counter will give it Coke instead of Diet Coke
when my illness goes with them it waits
till my friends are out of earshot and whispers
to the girl at the counter
I'm diabetic   please don't get it wrong

I ran for a long time with my illness and smoked
Dear Pillow my illness said I am empty as a packed lunch
Dear Pillow how many calories in a red flower
the pillow never did speak back

cat food Mars Bars bread
bread from the freezer pasta so much cake
bread from the freezer three types of cheese

The therapist suggests a self-help book for my illness
my friend's mum buys it   the self-help book
addresses my illness as She
sometimes it just wants to be scooped up
helpless and placed in a bathtub

My illness grew into itself so much that it ran one day
23 miles from my parents to my nan's house
trucks on a motorway
horns down Sunday lanes
across some shortcut cornfields and arrived
just in time for dinner

my illness is taking all of the red flowers
inside itself so the field is just filled with my illness
my illness taking all of this imagery
into itself until it is outgrowing
the place where it hides
my friends now speeding past in cars
ostensibly my father is downstairs sore to the dickens
about everything

Cake

When first I saw her lips meet another man's face I didn't think
Shit! I thought Cake   I thought a pink and iced castle cake stark
and alone in the garden rain   the party departed   its glowering
candle dumbstruck   one small flame tearing for the now moistening air
when first I saw her lips meet another man's face

I didn't think How could she do this to another man's face?
I pictured that big yellow bowl I pictured that brown wooden
spoon my mother used to stir its quickening mixture   its
mixture rolling further and further toward its intended self
when first I saw when first I saw her lips

I saw a warm sponge rise in the oven of my mother's kitchen
to meet its supposéd and predestined shape I saw it cut its well-
sprung figure I saw its proud stature and the icing on top and
my mother's   her gladdened hands in her apron   I thought Cake
when first I saw another man   her lips on another man's face

the party gone inside   my mother's work my mother's finely
crafted work the care she took   a wet cake in the garden

Worship Music

Accept all happiness from me

E. E. CUMMINGS

Tell her each time she marries him I don a scarecrow's hat,
some straw, a hole-pocked coat and lance maniacal
across redundant fields. There are no crows, of course,
they crept away. Awry, they sport no need of me;

they are her cake-beaked wedding guests, sequin-eyed
and squawking rows of big band music, the favourites:
Frank, The Duke. But though their ungloved wings are clutched
through arms of in-laws and everybody sings, tell her this –

that there are other birds; sparrows who, like me,
have no common song. They blink in trees,
then chirrup and squeak and coo and cry. Tell her:
each one a song unjoined by mate or mate's mate, but

as I bound they swim to me, one, then more,
like I again might raise my voice; another bird,
another, pitched upon my trunk, my throat, my lips.
A different note from all. I strut a marching-band of sparrows,

a single prayer of sorts, an instrument of benediction
to wedding songs, to random notes and other souls,
to open windows, lights left on, to empty homes.
A trumpet to the unsung, the void, the not yet known.

Self Portrait #2

A moon
& two chairs, broken
& a half-glass of milk
& a small red candle in a small red bowl
& two untouched spoons before a tall lattice window
& a poster of a square-fringed girl with a smirk and a paddle
& a corner of a room with a square-fringed girl, a smirk and a paddle
& me an old man spanked
next to no light flickered on him.

I hope this will explain everything:

I was young. In fact, I was six when I saw my dad
hit my mum, hard in the face.
I was playing that game, *Buckaroo*. Nobody moved,

then the donkey kicked and I ran to my room.
I was so angry I made a gun with two fingers, a thumb,
and shot my cat square in the head.

Scamp didn't flinch, just licked his right paw
and winked. And none of this counts, except
the next day Scamp was dead.

Until the Sunday you slapped me, I'd forgotten.
Please understand, I wouldn't touch you those last weeks
for that reason, for your sake. I'm sorry.

(Some Violence

Such behaviour represents efforts at 'making a claim to power where there are no real resources for power' in response to marginalisation in most social domains.

STEVEN ROBERTS, 'Boys Will Be Boys'

Hi

Tony Lewin
was the first boy to really let me know I was a human
he wore
a high-top in the early 90s
he wore
seldom any school uniform   At our failing school
his right knee to the front of my thigh
was a person I loved entering the room
then leaving again without saying Hi

Hi

I'm not going anywhere but you are human. I'm telling you now
so you don't need your own Tony Lewin
Imagine I looked at you this morning before you went off out
into the language of right knees
and you were beautiful

> [when a person
>   looks for long enough at another person
>   they swap insecurities]

Forgive me if I looked away too soon
please come back unharmed

*

This is me: kicking the fuck out of a pigeon. Gavin's there, laughing – his big chest is a god who lampoons the world. Throw it Up, he says, put it up there and I'll *Le Tiss it* ('Le Tiss' being a particular man known for his manner of stroking an object with his foot, 'Up' being a particular triangle of air). In Gavin there is no such tenderness. Now Up is filled with pigeon. Now several small triangles of Up are filled with several smaller bits of pigeon

and Gavin will go on doing this until he dies, and I will go on failing at not doing what he says for 18 months, meanwhile bits of me are producing and reproducing bits in me that will one day produce bits of my thesis

*

This is me: standing at a bus stop five/six steps away from three teenage gods, giant and kicking the fuck out of a rickshaw driver. He is small, eastern European. A woman arrives. A woman speaks calm to them. A woman gets dry-slapped. A rickshaw driver doesn't die today but if he has children they will know something bad happened and when their father comes home from the world he is no god.

*

There are so many right knees to avoid in this age. The right knee
of employment. This is me as a kid: not being a god in Levi Strauss & Co.
folding jeans and being told to fold more and sell more jeans.
    While sex gods sing to and tell women
about their own bodies on CD tracks, another god (no sex) says
I can go for my lunch

The right knee of the lunch hour

*

I can tell you   of how we all laughed
at the hot-dog cart flung   by the rival trader out
across the street   its small owner   his whole manliness shrunk
to the size of each sausage-shaped piece of meat
a shit ton of bread rolls in front of us kids in the street

Could speak of the shucked-off onions in the street
the rival hot-dog cart upright   its owner laughing at the small man
or   of my dad's pride dashed   across our back garden
the night he suffered a full fist in the face   his head knocked in our back garden
   the arm fat and hairy of our neighbour Henry   retracting over the fence
my dad's own eye swelled and black in the BBQ smoke of our back garden

and we could agree how these are the same somehow
cogs grinding in each man of the narrow world

masculinity as   our neighbour's red and hairy knuckle
masculinity as   my dad's head knocked back
as a small man cursing
as shucked-off onions in the street
masculinity as next morning
my dad smoking crossed-legged on the doorstep
waiting for Henry to leave for work

*

Masculinity as spelling out TITS with a found can
of spray paint crossing it out and spelling SHIT
then FUCK   as a goal sprayed
on the back alley wall in yellow paint
as boys abuse each other beneath it with a football
as one boy   slightly older   [me] holding another boy's
baseball cap to the threat of Henry's wall
making him do knuckle press-ups till he cries

*

Somewhere everyone is beating and biting everybody else
In Swindon Eric Cantona stamps down hard
on the floor of a midfielder's midriff
In other news refusing to sing
working-class love songs to other men
with other men and your dad is a type of violence
laughing in the back of your lungs
and knowing you will leave this arena for something
or knowing that you've already left it
cue: Degree   AHRC funding   PhD
scholarship for research on working-class men
and a shameful sort of understanding

[https://www.youtube.com/watch?v=tp4wEewrQdU]

On YouTube an educated man is telling a teenager that he is uneducated and will never amount to anything. The man, of course, is a teacher of English. The teenager is, of course, a student of English and of this man. The lesson of the English teacher stretches out beyond the realms of the denotative and into a rap battle where it remains denotative. This is the lesson of the English teacher: a series of right knees in the thigh of the student. A bourgeois essay about his body being read back to him. *Taste* is the title of the essay. *This is not your language [but] ne'ertheless you are understood by it.* This is one of the essay's positions. Moreover, *your mother is a slag.* The teacher says this, articulate, witty. *Everyone in this room has had his dick sucked by her.*

Aristotle naturalises unequal resources thus: 'Citizens are ruled by their minds/ slaves by their bodies.' Marx explains: 'Citizens' minds rule slaves' bodies.' Bourdieu: 'All are ruled by the value locked inside of language. The value of a particular group. The language of a particular group.' The English teacher: *Let me introduce you to the value inside the language of my particular group: I am better than you.*

Of course, when the teenager responds with violence it is cliché.
Of course, the teacher of English is wearing a suit and his hands
      casually in his pockets.

Moreover, this language finds you ridiculous. This is the overall
      conclusion to his thesis,
with which we are all bound to agree.

*

I saw a clip today on YouTube of an animal understanding being democratically
elected: the Subject of a Bull   a showground of people making it mean to them
          violence
naming its body *killer*   what it had meant to them since forever
in bull runs in stories in news articles they write to each other   in cartoons
for children: talking bulls whose nature is bound, fixed to muscle upon cartoon
          muscle
the body of this creature is an abject fantasy they are explaining now
they are collectively telling through their voices in the air to themselves
and to the man in the pit
and the man in the pit is standing and telling it to the bull

but the bull does not yet recognise itself by this word

They have suddenly set its horns on fire making themselves scared of it
the man in the pit saying: This is what you are made of
you have violence and fire writ on your turning muscles

          and the slow-breathing creature is thinking
pulling this name Bull in and out of its nostrils

and the man understands the creature further with flailing arms
helps it to understand itself with pit-sand thrown in its eyes

and OK suddenly it understands

the man: for a moment, a pulsing orgasm, lust hung in the air
cue: screaming; cue: the world has realised it was right all along
cue: the animal being taken to a place where they can correct its evil by sword

*

This is me: having the same fantasy over and over about football hooliganism. This is the fantasy: that all hooligans are not hooligans, or: that all hooligans *are* hooligans but hooligan simply means performance artist. Flash Squads. Bodies flung at each other in the public spaces of England. Unfunded, and enacting their own erasure. See the manner in which this screaming face returns the anxiety of its masculine counterparts, ejecting from its own lower-class throat the name 'other', the choral affect of abject vocabulary, at once a type of communal ownership-taking and rejection of the subjects' position. This is emphasised by the fist this one throws into the mind of that one, and the one his own mind receives. The right knee's sudden jerk into others' legs. These acts performed again and again across car parks producing frequencies of pitch at once erotic and volatile: the animal language of each movement articulates a shared meaning – these extant beings – the vulgarity of the lower-class bodies becomes the loss of control of the lower-class body becomes 'mob' or 'horde' becomes the unruly becomes the need to be managed and disciplined. O Hand of the Law ride in on horseback, batons raised. O knights of the state, beat down upon them, take them away so I don't have to look!

Hi

perhaps the ultimate realisation   of working-class male violence
is sitting at the dinner table of a celebrated poet
as his wife congratulates you   on your recent PhD
on representations of working-class masculinity with the joke
that you are a hooligan she means   if hooligan means not hooligan
not performance artist   but that you have by writing
of *socio-symbolic violence within dominant discursive values*
employed the socio-symbolic violence within dominant discursive values
to effectively murder your own working-class self
the joke is she says that now you understand words
like socio-symbolic and discursive values   and have a certificate
to prove it you cannot any longer be working-class within
        the dominant discursive values which have
enabled your socio-symbolic act and which no amount
        of erasure can erase)

II

ıl Expre:
on 2000E,

ı

allenger 300
tation CJ4
nallenger 604
ienom 300
allenger 601
ition II
on 2000LX
enger 60
' 60

The Politics of Birds

I cradle the stable device of this bird – breathe – unscrew its head
   from the ache   you know as its beak
stare straight at myself in your idea of its eyes   then tap
   out each bead into the palm of my hand   untie the elastic
beneath the description of wings   unfasten your concept
   of plumage   and pocket   one unstuck *feather*
after another   its flash of *tail*   the buff politic of its *body*   I crack
   into the nut you understand as its lungs
the unreal science of its gut you think makes the whole *bird* tick
   and all of its contents are mine – I'm taking the whole thing back

The Language

One thing I've learned is   if you are asking
    whether you might have the crows again   then you've already got them
They're drawing you into their conversation
    If you need to check and then keep checking to articulate this
    then *they've* got *you*   Can you see
in the corner of your eye their heads fallen back their beaks flapped open
    and laughing? This is the particular language of the crows   Don't Look
into their multiple throats
    as kind ladies with clipboards have said
    as kind men in their cardigans have said
Look at your feet think *Feet* do your feet not become hot-itchy
    or your fingers   think *Fingers* do they not tingle audibly

One thing I've learned is   stare at the freckles on your own face
    and tell yourself I like the freckles on my own face so loud
    your crows are not visible   don't open your mouth wide
One thing is   think of the most feelgood pop song   get right inside
    and bend its words to mean nothing bad will happen
and sing this all the way to the supermarket
    test the potatoes test the potatoes
    like you've seen real people do – hold them up
to the distinguishing light and squeeze: do not see a glittery wing
    do not imagine the head of a *body*   Instead become the man
who squeezes potatoes and then goes home and cooks them with salt
Occasionally potatoes will taste of crows – sing with more volume

Sarah Sarsaparilla

And, of course, we all lose it occasionally, watching the long slim story
of your body move lovely in its print pyjamas, in front of instructional
hip-hop videos, and, sorry, we (meaning me) are pulling you in our minds
flush to boys we've thought we'd like to be,

                               have connived you
in dreams flush at the ballet with some handsome lad, some actress, or we
       chance
to think you running straight on out to kiss the security guard at Tesco –
       a real roué – intent on having you
over when his daughter's in bed.

And wearing things to snag your interest –
make up, butt plugs, slim jeans…our dried out eyes,
dry as hard boiled sweets, as coughed up lungs or just plain dry,
we (meaning me) have pictured our old bodies reading your books in your
       literal shoes
found out by each feminist word

and we've strained to rake our hearts right back through school,
remembering how they're messed up, and fooled
about with, bullying themselves (meaning me) to pin upon you our own cad-
dish fuckeries, copping a real crop of pain, dad-
sized, from your clockwork handpicked kindness – please stay please don't
                  please don't let these things (meaning me)
                       get in your way

Sympathy for Toast

Made from the bread of Brit tongue the seed of words the chanced combinations of curlicues or noises could mean 'brioche' as lief as 'mother' they might mean nothing but from where we are down here we need to understand ourselves and each other so acquiesce to conventions like 'sandwich' or 'toaster' which are almost always beneficial to their inventors and it is factual to say that most toast is grateful to be told what it is what it isn't

Its loss of pungency its dried-out freedom a loafed dialogy carved into meaning by the discourse of (we call them) 'knives' decide which ones will be cut thick enough to be gifted the 'yolk' has often been an arbitrary symbol for imprisonment or slavery and is also the want by which toast understands itself (and it gasps) when the saucepan is rumbling is sometimes described as the process through which treacheries are bared but the toast thinks only of the prospect of the soft embrace of sticky yellow sun

Bred from the oven its enchantment with constructions of heat and light science has many positive things to say but seldom any about 'butter' is synonymous with 'sycophancy' to lubricate metaphorically and to batter into agreement with kindness to beat dynamically downward something through buttering but toast has nothing save the properties it is made from and cannot barter only hope that its colouring will carry enough currency just light enough a kind of tanned white gold is best to be chosen cut further and eaten

(i.m my father)

Grandfather, with Flowers

Oh Harold, is it true your eyes set loose a stream
of heart-shaped balloons and pink feathers
when you first saw her, that those balloons,
those feathers knit together to clothe her,

when she wore that knitted gown, your wink
turned the balloons to sequins, found reflected
in each an image of a celebration feast for her
and seven bridesmaids? Say it is and, Harold,

say it was the barley and hops that misled you,
the barley, the hops which curled your fist.
That when you slept yourself clean of their curse,
in your sleep those sequins were glass bowls

filled with goldfish, each one mouthing a letter
of her name, in your sleep you found the given day
when those letters rearranged themselves as vows
and after those vows were spoken, you commanded

the balloons' and feathers' dispersal. Say it's true
that but for the hops, Harold, but for the barley, she'd
have forever been courted by balloons and pink feathers
and never would purple roses have clouded her eye.

*   *   *

Self Portrait #3

Take a photo and hold it fast
to yourself, that part the polaroid
only half-sees: your punctum.

An image cannot wholly develop
unless it's caught between
yourself and the part of you it fakes.

Poem in Which

she always leaves
a bacon sandwich on the kitchen table,
a message scribed in ketchup beneath its upper rung of bread.
In which I swallow whole the note and never know it's there.
I spell *I'm sorry* with sodden clothes, with smiling too long and flower stems,
on my mistakes, as they are happening, all of them.
Poem in which my mother is maddened, not disappointed.

Poem in which all my mothers are maddened: the old ladies
smoking at bus stops, scanning bacon and bread loaves at Tesco,
under flapping umbrellas in King's Cross and High Barnet. Poem in which
I forget my umbrella, am not a failure and my mothers,
all of them, are pretty and called Margaret.
    In which the rain spells their name on me
and dry patches of escarpment.

Please understand

almost as if I had the hands
and the face and soul of a pig did I react
so strange to the thrill
of bacon in your mouth. O girl
(bite me, bite down hard), I have been so attracted
by this sumptuous queerness: your physical
threat, your appetite for flesh, the suicide logic
of you there, me here, in my kitchen – the willing ignorance
of seven steps or eight steps between us. What's
love – with its carbohydrate-led emotion,
its bread-like quality broken
up between bits of bacon in your teeth?
                    My proteinous heart,
it's burning in its trotters to get to you.

If I'm Ever to Find These Trees Meaningful
I Must Have You by the Thighs

Something kind of like this: yes – a farmer with a pipe. No –
it began with a village asking why. It began with an old man. It
began with a village asking why it was – for the sake of an old
man, his ruined heart, his view of things assembled like smashed
stained glass, the portraits of wives who'd slighted him. He
had a grey beard, I see it, and a limp. The broken teeth of the
morning always at his neck, but nevertheless rich. He was a
rich man. And this plot of land was his, handed down to him.

We'll start with him staring, sitting back on his land's nape and
staring as the broke-toothed morning breathed. Staring and
thinking [   ]. And this thought he stored, as he cradled these
spines, these sapling yews. He stabbed them in the ground,
into the perimeter of this, his land and made it square. The
village looked on, asked why it was. You wouldn't know this.
He did this. And coughing with each stab he knew he'd soon
be gone and with no sons. So he handpicked seven 'Men of
Trust'. Coughing, he told them *No drunk may stain, no child
yak, no dog may sour this place.*

The trusted men repaid his faith. They shone lamps through
each dawn's broken teeth into the nooks of this, his square and
kept it safe. And these trees did grow. These trees did grow,
they all joined hands and fog did swell and paint the grass. And
the old man died. The village looked on asking why it was. The
village danced in memory of him, held a fête each year to cele-
brate his wealth, his tragic life, his fate. This isn't it, though.
There was the fire. You wouldn't know. The fire that nearly
licked right through the square, but the village danced, it danced
and stomped the flames out with its muddied soles. And then
rejoiced. It felt saved. This isn't it, though.

The field was sectioned, cordoned off for seasons. The fête had whittled to a glass raised in a public house by those who knew. You wouldn't know. There were people, boys and girls, who never looked upon the outskirts of what we do now. Seasons. Then a wedding. Permission from a son of a son of a 'man of trust's' son. The trees held firm, held hands, the village danced and sang a song. *This is it!* they sang, *this is the reason / the reason for the actions / of that old man.* Hearts were mended. As the village sang, the trees absorbed the throb of words in their own chests.

Alas, the marriage failed. You wouldn't know. That isn't it, though. This is: this fog, this painted blanket. Us, shivering on each other, mouths miming words we're not sure of. The leaves grown heavy. The leaves nodding.

Why

She knows you're thinking   an April scummed with mud
and you stuck at something too-hard   and turned thin
at your worst   an April scummed with mud   she collared you there
dirty-heeled   and Thomas plays violin thirty nights better
than you've ever slept   she knows   you're thinking
and also your shins   and she stays when you stuck at something
drenched in red hair   thirty nights too hard and kisses
turned thin   at your worst you walk better
than you've ever slept   in your shins   she knows
and dark dirty-heeled   Thomas plays violin and through April
your teeth go too hard for her   your scummed shins
a straight thirty nights   bite themselves back and she's there
and then there   and wearing your shoes   and your shins and
how weird morning comes   drenched in red hair   all eyes
and teeth that bite themselves back

Pear Tree

Remember then the tree in its canopy of white,
its rotund fruit dappled in August, resplendent.
Remember the full volume, in August, of its Christmas fanfare:
erect and lovely and the singular partridge, the kirrr-icking soul
of it, at rest and contented to reflect back your gaze.
Remember this: you looked at each other so hard,
the tree's seed became rounder and you and the tree
became for a moment each other.
                              Oh it remembers you now,
in the rasp of bronchial winter. Now: its colours striped
and less, the great air cut to shapes through its oxidised bones.
Its beaked soul remembers you now, pecking from branch
to branch. Come back.

Lucky

Won't stop fully
watching you grow big on your bike in Vauxhall Park
your dimpled elbows a little too far forward
your bare knees doing god's work propelling you onward
it's raining a bit and I'm thinking
of the crocodiles I dreamt snapping me up
asleep early this morning
there were so many I couldn't count
chasing me in my little wooden boat
rowed out not that far but too far
and watching you grow now
from this distance
all of my sadnesses are lucky
so many I couldn't count
are marching on
this articulate moment
you on your sprayed-gold bike
is a celebration
is a very small girl with my face
is me feeling very alive
is I can still see from all this way
those sadnesses
filing toward my ridiculous boat with its oars
and someone perhaps you is singing
and the crocodiles
a thousand teeth on the cold water tonight

He left the body as fluids

drench a mattress. He left the body
with mutton chops.
He left it as I left the family home – slightly aggrieved
and having never tried Italian. Since then,
I've been mostly pretending
not to be him, eating pizza with knife and fork,
perfecting my tomato sauce – a drizzle of oil, tomatoes.
I've given that sauce to lovers and daughters.
They've given me part-compliments. I've given myself
to picturing me:
        dying like that. I've given that
mattress to the rubbish tip. That mattress left my hands
empty. That mattress left my hands like he left this world:
filthy with swear words.

Alarum

it's like you're on your complete own he said
   coloured by   how shall I say   some hour
when good things like swimming pools are closed off to you
and permanent loved ones they don't get
the nebulae of off-licence   of corner shop is your daylight
you're locked he said outside of wholly being alive   a feeling pinned
only to the outer body

   a person standing unnoticed but too close in the supermarket
   a man in the background of a family photo
   crossing the road too slow

you're out-of-step with the common ground and carrying yourself about
like a mutt   gone between lamp posts foreign in your overcoat
you're clumping in then out of shops
not entirely covered up   round a pond in the park for days
and without knowing it he said it's almost   how shall I say
   as if you have become that mutt   large against your own self and mute
under that extra-big and human coat you wear

   a lone man in a restaurant picking up putting down a spoon
   somebody smoking a cigarette then smoking a cigarette
   a thumbnail and finger pinching an arm for a long time

only others forever caught in that same hour recognise you
muteness in overcoats   unseen but seen by each other
this one he said I saw borrow scissors from a balloon shop go outside and
      burst
all its blown-up balloons   and she stopped once to know herself in me
   as does the one man drunk on the library steps
and the gabbling one
   the one swinging punches in the thin dark air

Short

The whiskey in my dad's bottle outlasts his body
I should be older than this by now
but the crushing simplicity of your hair
but I'm being played by Joseph Gordon-Levitt
in a movie about someone whose dad died
we could rob a bank here – I say in my American voice –
and he'd still be dead
but the wind is in our faces and yours looks
more masculine in this light
and mine has really quite white teeth and eyelashes
call me princess ask me something and laugh
stroke my cheek my dad is dead
but the upbeat pop soundtrack
and you catching glances at boys' tanned legs
in slow moving traffic
your body whistling through the streets now
anything about the shape of your face
with your feet naked on a dashboard
riding shotgun distracted
theorising bad TV
and armpits a couple of days unshaved
mine are as clean as a whistle oh god
crows do not line both sides of the road here
you are so definitely not at work
we've got ancient shotguns in the back
oh god for black comedy an urn and my dad's ashes
a half-bottle of whiskey oh god
for black comedy you reach for a shotgun
spot a crow and kill it
then nothing happens
then nothing happens
then it did

NOTES

'The air itself' (11)
was written for Mark Waldron.

'Everything is always sometimes broken' (16)
was written for Alex MacDonald.

'Please understand' (54)
employs the words ending each line of Tina Turner's 'What's Love Got to Do with It'.